Anxiety with Gratitude

This notebook belongs to

This little gratitude journal has been designed to help you put things into perspective when you're feeling overwhelmed. Studies have shown that expressing daily gratitude can have beneficial effects on your state of being. Feelings of hopelessness and gloom contribute to stress in your life, and taking a few moments to focus on the good in your life and around you, can help to bring back your sense of balance within.

Although gratitude does not completely remove anxiety, it is a natural form of inner awakening that helps you see past the things that are making you anxious. With constant daily practice, your perspective begins to shift until it becomes a way of thinking and being. Overall, gratitude fosters more positive feelings, and studies have found that with consistent gratitude over time, people have developed the ability to deal with adversity, build stronger relationships and found greater happiness in their lives.

Use this journal to list 3 things that you are grateful for each day, and slowly grow your daily practice to be what works for you. Keep it simple, and more than anything, enjoy the experience.

© 2019 Silver Kiwi Media

ISBN: 9781095857175

All rights reserved.

No part of this publication may be reproduced, distributed, or transmitted in any form or by any means, including scanning, photocopying, recording, or other electronic or mechanical methods, without the prior written permission of the author, except in the case of brief quotations embodied in critical reviews and certain other non-commercial uses permitted by copyright law.

Disclaimer: The Publisher and their Team makes no claim as to the replacement for any kind of therapy and do not offer medical advice. No part of these books replaces the advice of a professional. The Author and Publisher assumes or undertakes NO LIABILITY for any loss or damage suffered as a result of the use, misuse or reliance on the information provided in this book.

Today I am grateful for

Today I am grateful for

Today I am grateful for

Today I am grateful for

Today I am grateful for

Today I am grateful for

Today I am grateful for

Today I am grateful for

Today I am grateful for

Today I am grateful for

Today I am grateful for

Today I am grateful for

Today I am grateful for

_____
_____
_____
_____
_____
_____
_____
_____
_____
_____
_____
_____
_____
_____
_____
_____
_____
_____

Today I am grateful for

Today I am grateful for

Today I am grateful for

Today I am grateful for

Today I am grateful for

Today I am grateful for

Today I am grateful for

Today I am grateful for

Today I am grateful for

Today I am grateful for

Today I am grateful for

Today I am grateful for

Today I am grateful for

Today I am grateful for

Today I am grateful for

Today I am grateful for

Today I am grateful for

Today I am grateful for

Today I am grateful for

_____
_____
_____
_____
_____
_____
_____
_____
_____
_____
_____
_____
_____
_____
_____
_____
_____
_____
_____
_____

Today I am grateful for

Today I am grateful for

Today I am grateful for

Today I am grateful for

Today I am grateful for

Today I am grateful for

Today I am grateful for

Today I am grateful for

Today I am grateful for

Today I am grateful for

Today I am grateful for

Today I am grateful for

Today I am grateful for

Today I am grateful for

Today I am grateful for

Today I am grateful for

Today I am grateful for

Today I am grateful for

Today I am grateful for

Today I am grateful for

Today I am grateful for

Today I am grateful for

Today I am grateful for

Today I am grateful for

Today I am grateful for

Today I am grateful for

Today I am grateful for

Today I am grateful for

Today I am grateful for

Today I am grateful for

Today I am grateful for

Today I am grateful for

Today I am grateful for

Today I am grateful for

Today I am grateful for

Today I am grateful for

Today I am grateful for

Today I am grateful for

Today I am grateful for

Today I am grateful for

Today I am grateful for

Today I am grateful for

Today I am grateful for

Today I am grateful for

Today I am grateful for

Today I am grateful for

Today I am grateful for

Today I am grateful for

Today I am grateful for

Today I am grateful for

Today I am grateful for

Today I am grateful for

Today I am grateful for

Today I am grateful for

Today I am grateful for

Today I am grateful for

Today I am grateful for

Today I am grateful for

Today I am grateful for

Today I am grateful for

Today I am grateful for

Today I am grateful for

Today I am grateful for

Today I am grateful for

Today I am grateful for

Today I am grateful for

Today I am grateful for

Today I am grateful for

Today I am grateful for

Today I am grateful for

Today I am grateful for

Today I am grateful for

Today I am grateful for

Today I am grateful for

Today I am grateful for

Today I am grateful for

Made in the USA
Lexington, KY
28 June 2019